WORLD MYTHOLOGY

Second Edition

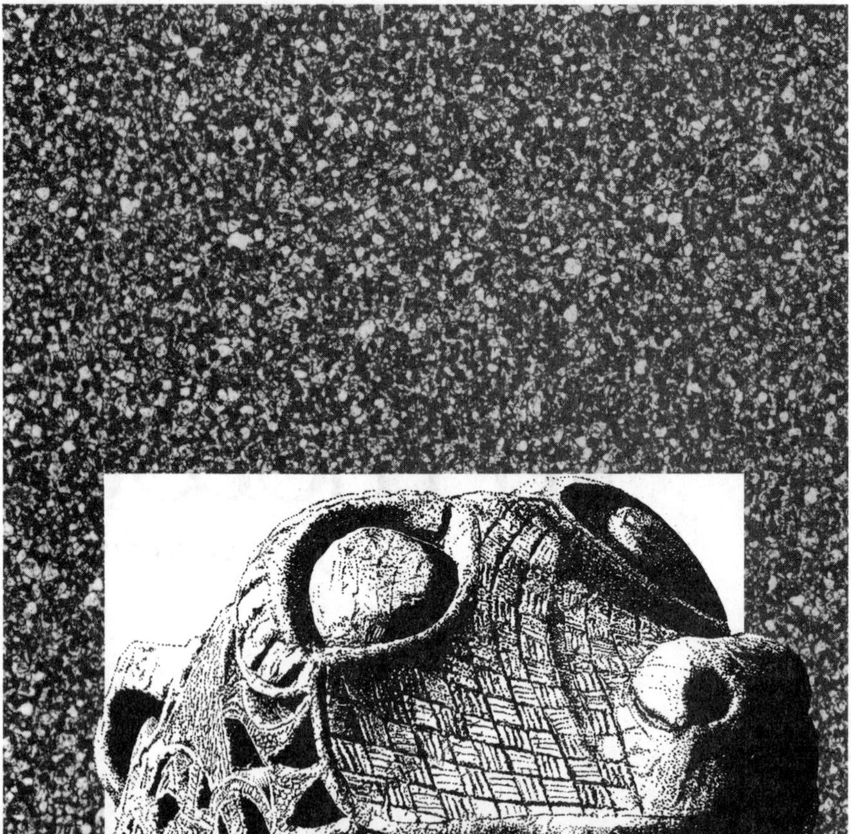